TEACH US TO PRAY

WHAT OTHERS ARE SAYING...

What an encouraging book! Rob's insight and wisdom is incredibly helpful – especially if you struggle a bit in prayer. I would urge you not to miss it.
Rob Parsons
Care for the Family

This delightfully written book flows from the life of a man who has learned to talk with God in the way Jesus taught his disciples to. It is devotionally inspiring and wonderfully practical, addressing head-on the challenges we all face in developing a healthy prayer life. Whether you have been following Jesus for 5 minutes or 50 years, you will be encouraged and helped by this profound yet accessible exposition of the People's Prayer.
Stephen Matthew
Resident Ministry at LIFE Church UK and Principal of the Building Church Academy

Rob is one of the most influential leaders in my life. Over the years his wisdom and encouragement have greatly helped me on my journey of faith. This book distils that wisdom and offers a fresh and practical insight into the Lord's Prayer that will give many Christians a new perspective on Jesus' teaching and a greater understanding of the power of prayer. I would highly recommend this book to anyone; it is a must read.
Ben Cooley
Co-founder and CEO Hope for Justice

If you were one of those first disciples of Jesus, what would you have asked him? 'Lord, please show us how to do miracles, how to walk on water, how to raise the dead, how to preach, how to share our faith...' I think those are some of the things I would have liked Jesus to have taught me. They didn't ask, 'Lord, teach us how to be better marriage partners or employees or employers.' They didn't ask him to teach them to be more successful or kind or wealthy, or for a better golf swing. But though they got so much wrong, like you and me, I'm glad they made that wise choice, like King Solomon once did, to ask for the best thing that secures every other important thing with it.

Nobody I meet ever says they feel like they spend too much time praying, or that they're too good at it. We all have our 'L Plates' on when we're on our knees. This book, by my dear friend Rob White, won't be the last word on prayer because there's always more for us to learn from Jesus, but it's certainly one of the first resources I will point people to who have that same, most important request to make of Jesus, 'Lord, teach us to pray.'
Anthony Delaney
Leader of the Ivy network of churches and New Thing Europe

Rob White is one of the most talented communicators in the Christian world today. He has a great gift of sharing through his own experience that we are not alone in facing the struggles of living out the Christian life. In this practical and accessible book he has made the subject of prayer – so often a source of feelings of guilt and failure – into something not only achievable in the daily life of a believer, but also a potential delight.
Richard Williamson
Founder/Leader of Epiphany Music Group

One of my first memories of Rob is an inspiring Spring Harvest seminar series on spiritual warfare back in the 1980s. He has

been a true man of prayer for many decades. This book has encapsulated his experience and will be a great encouragement to anyone seeking a close relationship with God and an effective ministry of prayer to bring his blessing to our needy world.
Celia Bowring
Prayer Co-ordinator, CARE

Rob writes as he speaks with authenticity and passion. *Teach us to Pray* is full of brilliant, practical suggestions inspiring a deeper desire for intimacy with God through prayer.
Sarah Jackson
HTB Group Chief of Staff

This book is a wonderful reminder of the delightful riches we can discover in prayer. Filled with honest wisdom and great humour, it will leave you hungry to pray more.
Revd Tom Jackson
Resurgo Trust

OUR
FATHER
WHO IS IN
HEAVEN
HALLOWED BE YOUR NAME
YOUR KINGDOM COME
YOUR WILL BE DONE ON EARTH AS IT IS IN HEAVEN
GIVE US THIS DAY OUR DAILY BREAD
AND FORGIVE US OUR DEBTS
AS WE FORGIVE OUR DEBTORS
AND LEAD
US NOT INTO
TEMPTATION
BUT DELIVER US FROM EVIL
FOR YOURS
IS THE
KINGDOM
AND THE
POWER
AND THE
GLORY
FOREVER
AMEN

TEACH US TO PRAY

Rob White

malcolm down
PUBLISHING

21 20 19 18 17 16   7 6 5 4 3 2 1

First published 2016 by Malcolm Down Publishing Ltd.
www.malcolmdown.co.uk

British Library Cataloguing in Publication Data
A catalogue record for this book is available from the British Library.

ISBN 978-1-910786-19-2

Cover design by Esther Kotecha
Cover image used under license from Shutterstock.com/Eleanormiv

Printed in the UK
by Bell and Bain Ltd, Glasgow

A BIT ABOUT THIS BOOK

I've been speaking on this topic for quite a number of years in many different places. People have asked me when I was going to put it in writing, none more so than a fellow trustee of Hope for Justice, Paul Davis, who's asked me every time I've seen him! For this I'm very grateful because it's prompted me to get on with it. Actually, my son-in-law Bruce Marshall had also said a couple of times that I should share whatever wisdom I have with a greater number of people. He may well overestimate my wisdom, but I appreciate the fact that he thinks I've got some! In the early days, I was encouraged to write by Rosh Ravindran, one of my friends in the leadership team of our church plant, Life Church Wilmslow. Obviously my thanks go to my wife, Marion, for bearing with me as I took on the time-consuming activity of writing and encouraging me along the way. I'm also most grateful to Robin Croxon, who helped me to see that writing this was possible and guided me in the process, as well as introducing me to the publisher. That publisher is Malcolm Down and I'm grateful to him and Sarah Griggs for being partners in this and producing the finished article.

My greatest joy would be that you would experience a similar transformation in your prayer life to that which has led to this book being written.

CONTENTS

FOREWORD

Rob White is one of the good guys. I can say that after being a friend and colleague of his for over two decades. He's also a guy who knows a fair bit about prayer. The teaching you will be reading in this book includes material that I have heard Rob deliver on a number of occasions and in various different settings, and I know that it is really, truly explosive stuff that if put into practice is nothing short of life changing.

Right now Rob is a trustee of the ministry I lead, *The Message Trust*, and recently has been encouraging me to take a fresh look at my job description to see if it is fit for purpose as the charity grows exponentially. I've said to Rob and the other trustees that my job description should really only have two lines:

• keep prayer hot
• keep mission hot

It's actually the job description of any church or ministry leader who has their head screwed on, because if we can do these two things then, in one sense, everything else should look after itself. That's why this book is so exciting, as I'm convinced that looking at the Master's model of prayer means that more than ever we will want to be in that sweet spot of mission and prayer that he modelled so beautifully.

Arrogantly enough, I actually believe that *The Message Trust* is a revival movement and I know Rob does too. He firmly believes that he will not die without seeing a major move of God amongst this nation's young people. Yet the truth is, every major move of revival has been pre-empted by and then fuelled by revival prayer and actually, when the prayer died down so did the revival. It really does make me want to say with the disciples, 'Lord, teach me to pray.' And here it is in your hands, an unpacking of perhaps the most important request that anyone could ever make.

So read on and feel free to get stirred, inspired and motivated to pray more regularly and more effectively. And as you do, you can be sure that you will find the Holy Spirit motivating you to go out and change the world. Maybe you will even find yourself equipped to be part of a major move of God amongst your nation's young people. Is there really anything more exciting than that?

Andy Hawthorne OBE
Founder of The Message Trust

1
SO YOU DON'T FIND PRAYER EASY?

Do you struggle with prayer? I certainly used to. And please don't think that I've arrived or that I am a mighty man of prayer. Don't get images of me prostrate on a cold, hard floor for hours, having started at 4.30 a.m. The truth is I still have prayer-less times in my life, but I have come to a place where praying itself is not a struggle.

That's the only reason I dare to write this book, because I've found something that I believe is worth passing on. You could well have found this too, because it's right there on the pages of Scripture. But you may not have realised just how helpful it is. However, before I get to the heart of things I want to outline my own journey so that you can see how this revelation came about for me.

During the time that I was National Director of Youth for Christ here in the UK, we sensed a call from God to pray for revival amongst young people. To that end we'd arranged a tour called 'Going for Glory', which we embarked on with other youth agencies and took to some forty venues. Each evening took the form of a prayer 'concert' – in other words a corporate prayer gathering with different methods of praying and times of worship.

At that time, I'd been elected to the board of YFC International and found that board meetings were held in different parts of the world and I needed to travel to Hawaii or Texas and other equally interesting locations. What a difficult prospect to face! Each time I had to spend hours in prayer before I could make a decision on whether I should go. (If you believe that you'd believe anything!) However, my first meeting was in Seoul, South Korea, and around that time the UK YFC board had granted me a sabbatical. The church in South Korea is well known for its prayer life, so I decided to take the sabbatical around the board meeting in Seoul and see for myself how the church's prayer life expressed itself.

I understood that the largest church in South Korea, if not the world, was Yoido Full Gospel Church, famous for its size and its 'Prayer Mountain', so I decided to spend whatever time I could there outside of our board meetings. I visited the church offices in the massive building to ask what time the prayer meeting was. 'Which one?' was the reply. I was told that there was a prayer meeting there every morning, except Sunday ('how unspiritual' I thought) when there were too many services to prepare for. Then there was a prayer gathering on a Friday evening that started at about 10 p.m. and went through to early Saturday morning.

I decided to go to that gathering with one of my colleagues. So we duly arrived at the church and were told to go to the upper levels. On the way up the winding stairs, we had brief glimpses on TV monitors of lively chatter amongst those gathering. We were shown to the foreign visitors' section, which alone had a few hundred seats, and were each handed a pair of headphones to plug into the back of the seat in front and choose which language we wanted for translation. As we took our seats, the event began and the lively chatter gave way to silence.

I remember it so clearly: the leader spoke briefly, announcing that their Senior Pastor was in Japan, believing God for a lively church to be raised up there. The leader then invited people with these words, 'Let us pray.' And with that, the thousands there – yes, thousands – stood and prayed aloud together. It was the first time I'd ever heard anything like it. It started like a river and grew into a torrent, and within minutes I was in tears, thinking that if God could do that there, surely he could do it in what seemed like the bland, too-safe environment of the UK.

Then it became personal, as I shed further tears, realising my poverty of prayer and lack of passion. I found myself crying, 'God, do it in me!' I have to admit that after about fifteen minutes my cynical side emerged and I wondered whether it was some kind of Eastern mantra with a Christian slant, and grew a bit colder to it. But after another five minutes the leader rang a little bell and everybody stopped moving about (there was a lot of physical expression around), fell silent and sat down. At that moment I sensed God leaning out of heaven and rapping me on the knuckles (please forgive memories of schooldays many years ago) saying, 'Don't ever judge in your flesh what I'm doing by my Spirit.' I felt rebuked and realised that my tears of longing were real and had been sparked by a true work of God's Spirit, both in the gathering and in me.

We couldn't stay for the whole night of prayer, as we had our first board meeting the next day, but we stayed for long enough to witness these twenty-minute bursts of corporate prayer for all sorts of different issues, interspersed with some singing and some testimonies. The one thing I knew was that something real had been awakened in me and that I had to build on it and not let it drift away once I was back home.

If that filled me with a desire to become a man of prayer,

the next encounter gave me a way to fulfil that. Because of my sabbatical, I was able to then go to the US where I spent a few days in a church I'd heard of which also had a real 'prayer movement'. They gathered every morning (well, at least those who wanted to) at 6 a.m. for an hour. People would come before work and would spend the first half an hour praying individually somewhere in the room. The other half an hour was given to corporate prayer, using what we know as the Lord's Prayer as the template for guiding the time of prayer.

A young man had been assigned to pick me up from the hotel, guide me etc., and one morning as we were doing the individual praying I sensed him sidling up to me. I was kneeling, so he knelt down beside me and whispered, 'Can I stay beside you because I've never prayed near a mighty man of God from the UK before.' If only he'd known that, being in a strange place and only just having sensed this work of God in me, I was struggling to pray as passionately as it seemed others were. In all honesty, I felt as though I couldn't let him down, so I started to pray with passion and fervour. However, much of it was done on purpose rather than from the heart, so although in one way it was an amusing incident, it was actually a very challenging one.

After these ten days I arrived home, concerned that maybe what had happened in me would disappear as I got on with life as usual. Haven't you often felt like that? You sense God has spoken to you or done something in you and you've welcomed it, but you have this fear that it might vanish or drift away. I vowed to build on what God had done rather than risk it seeming to disappear. I do believe that God's work in us stays, but if we don't exercise it, it will seem to go.

I began to find myself looking forward to my prayer times, as I sensed I really was meeting with the Father. It was a big change – and it wasn't just miraculously worked by God, I had to build on what had happened. I'll unfold what has helped me a little later in the book, but I do want to say that the starting place is the same for all of us.

Christopher Robin – do you remember him? There's a poem called 'Vespers', by A.A. Milne who created Winnie-the-Pooh, that you may remember from your childhood or you may have read to your children. On my journey of wanting to be a man of prayer, for some reason this poem came to mind.

It starts with the words, 'Little boy kneels at the foot of the bed . . .' It goes on to describe how Christopher Robin, obviously tired, kneels by his bed and prays for a number of things, in much the same way as our own children might do – though whether they'd kneel by the bed any more is highly doubtful! He prays for – in his words – his mummy and daddy and his nanny. His mind wanders on to completely different things which have nothing to do with prayer and he has to keep coming back to praying for the next thing, on what it seems must be his usual list.

At one stage, with his head in his hands, he peeps through his fingers and is immediately distracted by what he sees in front of him. That sets him off thinking about something else. He ends by remembering to pray for himself – that God will bless him. It's a cute picture of a child praying, and whenever I look at it, I remember my children praying when they were little. Nostalgia grows as you get older!

Children's prayers are cute, aren't they? They often don't contain correct theology, but do have a lot of heart. I remember one family car journey years ago, when our daughters were small, when one of them exclaimed, 'Daddy, Jesus is at home today!' On enquiring as to how she arrived at that conclusion she responded, 'I can see his blue dressing-gown hanging on a cloud.' No marks for theology; full marks for heart. Christopher Robin, in the poem, follows a childish train of thought expressed in very simple requests.

This poem challenged me because I realised that actually my praying was not dissimilar to Christopher Robin's. I used longer words and had more varied requests, and at times gave praise to the one I was praying to, but actually my prayer life was not much more than praying by rote for the same things each time, with little passion, imagination or even expectation that the prayer would be answered.

In fact, I rewrote the first and last verse like this:

Grown man sits in a chair by the bed,
Into his hands droops a sleepy head.
Hush! Hush! Speak loudly who dares!
Dad fell asleep while saying his prayers.

I guess you've been there as well. When we do rise from our prayerlessness and try again, it seems that tiredness and wandering minds too easily hijack our efforts. Maybe you can also relate, as I did, to the open fingers that I mentioned. Many times my mind has wandered and, with head in hands, I spot something through my open fingers and start thinking of something else entirely. I berate myself for losing concentration in the most important act of communicating with a mighty God.

These are just a few of the many reasons why I needed to

understand how to pray. I realised that, however many books I read and sermons I listened to on prayer, although I was challenged, perhaps rebuked, I was making minimal progress.

And so the journey that I outlined at the beginning of this chapter began. Much of what I write in this book is about how I came to find prayer much more meaningful – a delight – and my trust is that you will find the same also. But before I get there, I want to say a few foundational things about prayer so that you, the reader, and I, the author, have a basic understanding in common.

2
WHAT IS PRAYER ANYWAY?

I said that I wanted to make some general points about prayer so that you and I achieve some common basic understanding. I think this is important, as it leads into the heart of what I want to pass on.

Firstly, a few points from Matthew 6:5–8:

'And when you pray, do not be like the hypocrites, for they love to pray standing in the synagogues and on the street corners to be seen by others. Truly I tell you, they have received their reward in full. But when you pray, go into your room, close the door and pray to your Father, who is unseen. Then your Father, who sees what is done in secret, will reward you. And when you pray, do not keep on babbling like pagans, for they think they will be heard because of their many words. Do not be like them, for your Father knows what you need before you ask him.'

Private before public prayer (vv. 5–6)

Prayer can be showy. You've probably been in prayer gatherings where someone prays a long prayer using flowery language. I often wonder whether that person has much of a personal devotional life – probably because that's what I used to be like. I know I shouldn't tar people with the same brush, but I have also learnt that, as with anything in life, I'm not the only one. Prayer is not entertainment; it's a time of fellowship with God.

The place of prayer (v. 6)

Yes, I know you can pray anywhere. God doesn't rule certain locations out of bounds. But there is something about having a place where we pray regularly. I've found that to be really helpful. As I have already said, as I grew in my new-found zeal for prayer I began to find myself looking forward to my prayer times, sensing that I really was meeting with the Father. The room in which I prayed became synonymous with those times, and I would go to the room expectant that I was going to meet with God. The result was that I approached my personal prayer times with faith.

It's not about quantity (vv. 7–8)

Praying for a long time, using many words or repetition doesn't mean we are more likely to get God's attention. I really don't know why we feel that God will hear us more clearly like that. This Scripture makes it clear that it's not about words, length or repetition, because God knows anyway. It's about quality – the right heart attitude, concentrating on what we're doing, trying to live a life that doesn't contradict our prayer life – not quantity.

As I make a few more general points, let's do something a bit different. I'll make some statements you might hear about prayer, and you can respond with 'right' or 'wrong' or 'I'm not sure; could be a bit of both'. I'll then give my response and the reason why.

Statement 1: If I don't pray in the morning, God won't bless me so much during the day.

What's your response? Mine is 'wrong'. God's blessings aren't contingent on the things we do, as we know. We know we can't earn our way to God or his generosity. But if we're honest, we also acknowledge that those thoughts do arise in us from time to time and we start trying to work harder or do better so that God will take more notice. And we think that if we don't pray enough things could start going wrong. All of God's blessings are from his grace – they can't be earnt. However, there is one thing that needs to be said: if we do pray at the start of the day, we will have more faith to recognise and appropriate the blessings when they come.

Statement 2: If I pray more, my spiritual life will grow more.

Surely, in contrast to the response to the first statement, the response is 'right'. If our prayer life is having fellowship with God, then being in his presence must draw us closer to him. It's the same in any relationship – the longer we spend with someone the better we get to know them and the more the things they do and think rub off on us. Prayer and Scripture reading are our spiritual food, necessary for nourishment and growth.

Statement 3: I don't need special times of prayer; I'm in touch with God all day long.

If your response is 'I'm not sure', I can understand why. Surely if you really are communicating with him during the day, nothing can be better? But my response is 'wrong'. Why? You would probably say that Jesus was in touch with his Father all day long.

I'm sure he was, but he went off by himself, often, for times of prayer. If he did, surely we also need to.

Statement 4: I don't pray a lot because I don't have the ministry of intercession.

Well, you know the correct response is 'wrong' – and you're right. But it may just be that you've thought a bit like that. Maybe you've not put it like that, but somehow you feel you're not very good at praying and reckon that God will understand. You know other people who seem to be gifted pray-ers, so it's probably best to leave it to them. It's not that you never pray, but it doesn't form any meaningful part of your life. If prayer is communing with God, then you don't need a gift or ministry for that. You just need to get on with it!

Statement 5: Prayer is exceedingly difficult.

I can almost hear the response echoing loudly around the readership: 'right'. But let me surprise you with my response, which is 'wrong'. Please follow my logic here as I explain. Would you say, looking at Scripture, that prayer is a command or a suggestion? Surely it's a command. Ok, if that's so, let's see what the Bible has to say about God's commands: *'In fact, this is love for God: to keep his commands. And his commands are not burdensome'* (1 John 5:3). There you have it: his commands are not a burden; they're not difficult. Therefore, prayer is not difficult. The problem is that so many of us feel it is or find it is. If the Scripture (and, dare I say, my logic) is correct, then we should not find prayer difficult. 'Ok,' you say. 'Help me with that.' Well, that's the point of this book, but here's my immediate response. I call it '3D praying'.

Let me explain 3D praying to you. The three Ds stand for **Desire**, **Discipline** and **Delight**. First, and you cannot bypass this starting point, there needs to be **Desire**. Desire to be a person of prayer. Without that desire, nothing will ever change. You can't force the desire, but you can ask God to plant that in you by his Spirit. That's what happened to me during those times in Korea and the US. You don't need to go there or anywhere else to receive this touch from God. In fact, if I'd been challenged at the right time back in the UK, I could have asked God there and then for that desire.

Second, it requires **Discipline**. Actually, you could double the D and make it daily discipline. This is the hard part, as you've probably already discovered. But I want to assure you that as you face the discipline it gets a lot easier; you'll find the third D eases it considerably. Here I need to reiterate my honest admission that I still have prayer-less times in my life. However, now they're not because prayer is a struggle for me, but because I don't discipline myself (during busy periods or doing my own thing) to make the time. I'm the loser, and I know it.

The third D is **Delight**. Yes, truly prayer has become a delight for me: spending time with the Father, opening up my life with its ups and downs, hearing what he has to say to me. What's not to like! That means that I can look forward to praying; making my way towards the place where I usually pray I'm actually expectant that I'll meet God during that time. What a change! It's delightful.

I really believe that you can experience this change as well if you want. Maybe you already have a strong prayer life. What I'm going to explain as we proceed does not in any way negate that or suggest that it's wrong. This is primarily for those who freely admit that they struggle with prayer.

Statement 6: Prayer is asking God to do things for us.

If your response is 'I'm not sure', you would be in good company because you realise that this is part of prayer, but not the whole. However, as a statement without qualification, my response to it must be 'wrong'. Maybe I'm being pedantic, but I'm being so in order to make what I consider to be a most important point. As I mentioned in the first chapter, much of our praying can be by rote and little more than series of requests. But surely that's missing the richness of prayer. We've been invited and welcomed into God's presence not just to present a few requests, but to spend time enjoying him, listening to him and learning from him. Let me put it this way: prayer is not me asking God into my world to solve my problems, but God asking me into his world to serve his purposes. It's a bit like being in a military operations HQ (I would imagine), where you would get an overview of the battle or exercise and receive orders regarding the part that you are asked to play. Obviously, within that, questions can be asked and requests made. But in that place, I'm caught up in something much bigger than me.

Statement 7: True prayer needs to be learnt.

What's your response to that? I guess most readers will hesitate, then opt for 'wrong'. If so, I believe you'd be wrong. I believe that the correct response is 'right'. Everything that I'm going to say from this point on comes from the understanding that prayer needs to be learnt. Not diploma or degree course learning, but a realisation that we need to receive wisdom. This has been the starting point in my journey of prayer – and it's not a secret upon which I stumbled, but revelation from a well-known Scripture, Luke 11:1:

One of his disciples said to him, 'Lord, teach us to pray, just as John taught his disciples.'

Let's stop there for a moment. Here's a request from a disciple who has been present whilst Jesus was praying (the verse begins with that) and wants to learn. What does Jesus reply? 'Don't waste my time. You should know that prayer is just chatting with the Father. Surely you know that simple song, "A little talk with Jesus makes it right, all right," so go and do it'? Of course not! Jesus responds by teaching them how to pray. As with all Jesus' teaching, if it's good for those who heard it first-hand, it's also good for us.

What have we done with that teaching? Most of us know the prayer he taught and might say it occasionally, but have not stopped to consider it in any more depth. We struggle with prayer, but haven't been to the seminar that Jesus gives on the subject. We've probably been to all sorts of seminars at all sorts of events, possibly on subjects like spiritual warfare, gifts of the Spirit, how to lead worship, family life, etc. but have overlooked this one teaching of Jesus that came as a result of someone asking to learn. My thesis is that if you struggle with prayer, you'd better start with hearing what Jesus has to say on the subject. Interestingly, nowhere else in Scripture do we read of the disciples asking Jesus to teach them something. They probably did, but those words are not recorded. Here's the one time when that happened and Jesus responded, and we either ignore it or overlook it. Crazy!

In the next chapter, I want to look at why this prayer is so useful for those of us looking for help.

3
THIS MAKES ALL THE DIFFERENCE

So here's the prayer. It's known as the 'Lord's Prayer', but my contention is that the Lord's prayer is in John chapter 17, where he prays a passionate, heartfelt prayer. I've renamed this prayer the 'People's Prayer', because it's for you, for me, for couples, families and churches everywhere. We find it in two places in the Bible – Luke chapter 11, and Matthew chapter 6. Maybe Matthew and Luke remembered this occasion and recorded it in different ways, or maybe Jesus taught it twice. I think that's just as likely, as the context is quite different. However, that's not of major significance. The significance and importance lies in the fact that Jesus teaches this prayer as the way to pray. We've already seen that in Luke he's responding to a request about how to pray; in Matthew it's recorded that he said, *'This, then, is how you should pray'* (6:9). In neither place is it a mere suggestion or a kind of 'give this a bash' statement – it is very directional.

Some could be thinking, 'Hey, that's good, it's a short prayer so I can do that easily.' Not so fast! Do we really think that Jesus taught us to pray with something that can be rattled through in a few seconds? The problem is that this prayer is well known to most of us, and is said or sung in many places with no further thought. It is often used like a kind of mantra. So it becomes fairly meaningless.

Here's what Jesus was doing. The rabbis in Jesus' day taught people 'index praying'. You know what an index is – it appears, usually at the beginning of a book, giving chapter numbers and titles (although I suppose more correctly called the Contents). Imagine using a large book for any study or work you're doing and finding there's no index. How would you find your way around? On the other hand, what if there were just an index and no substance to the book? The point of the index is to act as a pointer to the substance.

That's exactly what index praying was all about. The rabbis would provide the points for prayer, like an index, and the people would fill in the substance – their own prayers. This is the method Jesus was teaching in this prayer. Can you now see the People's Prayer like that? And what an index of titles! I guess you can glean your own index from the prayer, but here's mine (see Fig. 1):

1. Worshipping the Father
2. God's kingdom
3. God's will/guidance
4. Our daily needs
5. Forgiveness/relationships
6. Spiritual warfare

I challenge you to find one subject, broadly speaking, that's not covered in this prayer. No wonder Jesus taught it! Hopefully you can begin to see why it's such a great prayer to pray and how it can help you in your prayer life.

	GOD/MAN/ENEMY	
Man's heart open to God		Worshipping the Father
		God's kingdom
		God's will/guidance
God's heart open to man		Daily needs
		Forgiveness/relationships
		Spiritual warfare

Fig. 1

I've often wondered what prompted the disciples to ask Jesus to teach them to pray. Was it because they watched him praying, probably aloud but fairly quietly, and wondered what he was saying? Or – and this is my guess – did they see the way that Jesus lived, hear his amazingly wise teaching and the many miracles he performed, and wonder where the power came from? Did they think that the power stemmed from his time spent with the Father in prayer? If so, then no wonder they said, 'Teach us to pray'!

Maybe it's already obvious, but I'd like to give some reasons why praying in this way is so helpful. Firstly, we're obviously praying according to God's will – and that's something with which I often struggled as I read the verse that says, *'This is the confidence we have in approaching God: that if we ask anything according to his will, he hears us. And if we know that he hears us – whatever we ask – we know that we have what we asked of him.'* (1 John 5: 14–15). How could I be sure that what I was praying was according to his will? Surely I must have been praying according to his will if I was praying the prayer he gave.

Secondly, this prayer covers everybody with whom we have to deal, i.e. other humans, God and, although not any means by choice, the enemy of our souls (see Fig. 1). So it's complete in that sense.

Thirdly, the prayer is structured so that it's not all about worshipping God, but includes our living needs. The first part is man's heart open to God and the second is God's heart open to man (see Fig. 1). By using this prayer, we can be sure that we are covering every area of life. If you want to learn about prayer, as those early disciples did, then here you have a lesson straight from the King of Kings.

There are also practical reasons why this prayer is so very helpful. Using the People's Prayer aids my concentration. I alluded to my own lack of concentration and wandering mind whilst praying, in Chapter 1. As I follow the structure, I know where I am and it keeps me engaged. Moreover, if I start the day with some prayer but, as often, too quickly run out of time, I can put an imaginary bookmark in the place that I stopped, or note the 'topic' in the 'index', and pick it up again at some other time without repeating myself or trying to recall where I'd got to.

4
IT'S ALL ABOUT FATHER
~᛫᛫~

So let's make a start with the prayer itself. You know the first line as well as I do, *'**Our Father** in heaven, hallowed be your name'*. We'll stop right there because that beginning makes all the difference to our prayer lives. It certainly did with mine and, because Jesus taught it as the way to pray, it will with yours!

The context in which we're praying affects our mindset and language, our hopes and expectations. If our prayers are primarily addressed to 'Great God', 'Mighty Lord' or 'Majestic Creator' (all of which are theologically correct), then our mindset can be one of daring to come before such majesty and greatness and hoping we'll be heard. We might even have a kind of pleading sense, much like a servant begging his king for a favour.

But Jesus tells his disciples that the way to pray is to our Father. And by Father, he doesn't mean just another title, but a relationship. So the context in which we pray is the context of family, where we as children approach a loving father. I realise as I write that for some the word 'father' falls as a hollow thud, because your experience of earthly fatherhood was not a good one. However, apart from finding release from the grip of that limitation you can, I trust, at least recognise that there is such a thing as good fathering, and that if the Bible is right about God being a father, then he would be a perfect one.

Within a relationship, we know that we are in a safe place. We're not pleading with a great deity who may or may not be interested, which can be the background to our praying, especially when we know all too well our sinfulness and failings, even though we've been taught that God *is* interested.

Let me illustrate by giving a possible, but most unlikely, scenario from a number of years ago. Let's say Prince Charles was addressing a public meeting and you were in the audience. As he makes quite a forcible point, you begin to stand up because you have something to say. Suddenly you find two men in suits bundling you firmly but quietly out of the door. You realise that they are security men and they ask, 'Why were you moving out of your seat towards His Royal Highness? You're a risk to security, so you'll be held in a secure room here until the meeting is over.' Afterwards, you hear that two young boys suddenly got out of their seats and ran up to where the Prince was standing. One tugged at his right trouser-leg and the other at his left, obviously wanting to get his attention. He looked down at them and said, 'William! Harry!' Ok, they're special people, but why can they get away with what you couldn't, even though your movements were misread?

The answer is that fatherhood means *access*. In other words, *I'm invited*. It also means *acceptance – I'm welcomed*. Furthermore, it means *attention – I'm heard*. Do you see how praying in the context of the child–Father relationship puts the whole thing on a different footing?

Maybe you've always wondered how other people manage to pray with purpose and passion. You've heard them, seen them, but your prayer life seems rather sterile in comparison. By praying aright, we can find that purpose and passion ourselves.

We live just south of the city of Manchester where, as you will probably know, there are two well-known football teams. The home of one of them is Old Trafford. Now, at the risk of losing friends and readers, I have to confess to not being interested in football. My sporting interest, at least from the armchair, is rugby, so I had never trodden the hallowed turf of Old Trafford. However, a friend asked me one day if I'd like to go. I agreed, but only because the England Rugby League team was playing Australia. As I approached the ground, I was aware of the excitement and anticipation mounting as the crowds chatted away. Suddenly we were there at the turnstile – the first 'click' bringing me to the ticket office window and the second taking me into the ground. Only then did I realise what all the fuss was about. The atmosphere was great and I was now part of it, rather than just looking in from the outside or merely hearing stories about it.

That's similar to the change in my prayer life. I used to be an onlooker only, hearing about people who prayed passionately, but then I became part of the action, as it were, through entering the 'ground' of praying to my Father (a relationship, remember, not a title). And let me add here that just as my entrance to Old Trafford through that turnstile was based on payment, so our entrance to the Father's presence has been purchased by Jesus Christ.

I want to be practical in this book, so I'm going to occasionally describe my own way of praying. It may not suit you at all, but the illustration might help more than just stating the truth behind it.

When I pray, I spend quite a time on the Father part. I often repeat quite a few times, 'Father, our Father, my Father!' and variations of that – not as some kind of mantra, but as statements of truth – and then speak out my amazement that I should be able to call God 'Father' and that he sees me as a son. I contemplate the truth of it, and often stay with it until the wonder of it dawns. I then feel ready to move on, by which time my faith has grown enormously, so the rest of the prayer time is built on real expectation.

It may be that you are not able to spend the length of time you sense would be needed to pray the way I've just described. The good news is, it's not about time, it's about heart attitude. I'm really not saying that the way I do it is 'the right way' and will bring magical answers. I am only painting one person's picture of being at prayer, so that you can see possible practical steps for yourself. However, it is based on solid theological truth.

Remember what I said in Chapter 3 about the order of this prayer that Jesus taught us: that there are the two sections – man's heart open to God, then God's heart open to man? So here we have opened our hearts to our Father and renewed, as it were, the relationship with him. Now we move on to recognise his all-powerfulness.

'*Our Father **in heaven***'. Actually, in Scripture there are very few references to a place called 'heaven'. Usually the word is plural – heavens – so it is essentially, 'Our Father in the heavens'. Please don't be concerned that the idea of heaven as you've always understood it is somehow being undermined. Not at all. Rather, I believe the idea of God being Father in 'the heavens' is much richer. So what does it mean?

Let's look in Scripture and see if we can find out how many heavens are recorded there. People talk about being in 'seventh heaven' and wonder if that has some possible root in Scripture, but of course it doesn't. However, in 2 Corinthians 12:2 we read, *'I know a man in Christ who fourteen years ago was caught up to the third heaven.'* He goes on to say that he was caught up to paradise. So we're on pretty safe ground to say that the third heaven is, if you like, the dwelling place of God and all heavenly beings.

How about the other two heavens? I'm no expert on space, so my explanations are very simple. I believe the first heaven is that immediate atmosphere around us, an expanse stretching some forty miles out, containing the air that we breathe, where birds and planes fly. The second heaven, then, is what we call the Milky Way, outstripping the best explorations of man, where the stars and planets exist.

When we pray, 'Our Father in the heavens', we are talking to one whose power operates from the ground up or the highest point of the heavens down. In other words, there is not one part of the universe we know (and that which we don't know) that is outside of the involvement and influence of our Father. That must have great bearing on our faith as we pray, realising that nothing is beyond our Father's scope.

Let me illustrate. Marion, my wife, and I have three daughters. Imagine that they are all around the age when they first learnt to drive. The three of them come to me one day and, having delegated the responsibility of voicing their request to the oldest one (only older by 20 minutes – yes, two of them are twins), they stand in a line in front of me. Jo, the oldest, begins, 'Dad, you love us don't you?'

'Yes,' I respond, 'you know I do.'

'Ok, Dad, we know you do, so we've got something to ask you.'

'Go on,' I say, getting increasingly suspicious.

'Well, Dad, would you please get each of us a brand new white Porsche Carrera.'

After picking myself up from near collapse in disbelief, I say, 'Sorry, girls, I can't possibly.'

By the way, I don't think anything like that would have happened but, as you probably know, children's requests can often be unrealistic.

See, I'm a loving father, but I can't meet the request; God is a loving Father and **can**. Not the Porsche necessarily! Hopefully you've got the point: we pray to a loving Father who is able to meet any request we put to him, because he's Father in the heavens. Doesn't that build faith as we pray? Remember the things that are coming later in the prayer. This opening means that we pray the rest in real expectation. Obviously I'm not saying that we're guaranteed to receive everything we ask, because we often ask with wrong motives or we don't pray in accordance with his will, but our attitude is a positive, faith-filled one.

There's one word in this first phrase that I've not yet talked about. It's the word '**our**'. Notice that there are no singular personal pronouns in the prayer. It's all 'our', 'we' and 'us'. Many of us were brought up with a very individualistic view of faith and Scripture. It was all about me – that Jesus died for me, God has forgiven me, I'm bound for heaven, etc. When we read Scripture in the light of community, we realise that most of it is addressed to us corporately. Obviously that doesn't take away from the personal, because the corporate is made up of individuals, but it should affect the way we believe, live and pray.

I would go so far as to say that if our prayers are 'us-less' they're close to being useless, because if my praying is centred around only me, I'm not praying according to the Father's will. Look again at the words that Jesus teaches. Whilst the things I pray there affect me personally, they are all totally connected to the world in which I live, where, as a follower of Jesus, I am deeply concerned about and involved in the lives of others.

I'm not saying that God won't hear us or that our prayers will not be answered, but I am saying that there's something wrong with our hearts and attitudes if we pray only selfishly. And how good to know that as we pray we are part of an international and cosmic family, each one having God as our Father. So many sisters and brothers! (Don't dwell too much right now on those last five words. You may currently be experiencing a few problems with one or two brothers and sisters.)

Having now recognised again the great privilege of being a child of the heavenly Father, we move on to the next part of the prayer.

5
A NAME FOR ALL SITUATIONS

So we've entered our prayer time by acknowledging our relationship with our heavenly Father who has all power and authority. Now we spend time worshipping him. That's not surprising, is it? That's part of the reason that this prayer is so brilliant – because there's an order to it. It would be wrong to move straight on from a deep, personal acknowledgement of God's fatherhood to a list of our needs. More about that later.

I'll be using 'your' rather than 'thy' as we go through. Part of what has made this such a formal, ritualistic prayer is that, although most of us have been calling God 'You' rather than 'Thee' for quite a time, we suddenly revert to 'Thee' and 'Thou' when it comes to the People's Prayer. Instead of the wonderful freedom in praying to a great Father that this prayer teaches, we get all religious about it. Why has it been elevated to this lofty, almost remote place, when the whole idea was to show ordinary disciples how to be honest and open with a majestic God?

As you look at Matthew 6 in the original Greek, you find that the thrust of verses 9 and 10 is this: *'hallowed be your name, [on earth as it is in heaven]'*; *'your kingdom come, [on earth as it is in heaven]'*; *'your will be done, [on earth as it is in heaven]'*. In other words, when we pray 'hallowed be your name', we are not merely saying, 'your name is hallowed (or holy)', but asking that his name be hallowed or made holy here on earth, as it is in heaven.

That immediately shows us how to pray this particular part of this prayer. Of course, we can worship him because his name is holy, but we are asking that his name is made holy, set apart, here on earth, in just the same way as it is in heaven. So what does that mean for our praying? Well, maybe an illustration will help.

I had the privilege of attending a public school (you'd probably never know it if you met me!) where all the teachers were men and all had graduated from either Oxford or Cambridge University. It was an all-boys school. Fights were common amongst the students, whilst a few kept an eye out for teachers or prefects. There were two students, well known to me: one of them, we'll call him Jim, was 'one of the lads' and the other, we'll call him Henry, was more of a boffin type. It would have been unthinkable that Henry would ever dream of getting into a scrap with Jim. However, there was one occasion when Jim, for some reason I've forgotten, was rude about Henry's parents. 'Say that again,' said Henry. Jim repeated what he'd said. Those of us who were near couldn't believe our ears when Henry said, 'Meet me in the playground at lunchtime.' Wow, a fight! And between the two most unlikely people. Many of us turned out to watch. I did wonder about offering to step in and try to stop it, but decided to stay towards the back of the crowd.

I'd heard Henry criticise his parents, so why did he get so mad when Jim was rude about them? Because however many times he may have been annoyed or angry with them, and been critical of them in front of his peers, he was not going to let someone else take their names in vain. After all, they were his parents, and actually, unsurprisingly, he loved them. How passionately do we defend the name of Jesus? Or do we let his name be derided, belittled, and treated as a joke without saying a word? If we pray, 'hallowed be your name,' surely we must be prepared to stand up for it! So our prayer is asking that the names of God and Jesus become holy names here on earth, treated with reverence, dignity and respect.

It's often said that there are three types of answer to prayer: 'Yes,' 'No,' and 'Wait.' I believe there are four answers: the three above and 'Do it yourself'. There are times when we ask for things when we should just get on and do it. Sometimes we use praying about something as an excuse for inaction. Obviously I realise that prayer and action go together, but I think you know what I mean. Surely, much of the People's Prayer **calls for** that – although it's how we're taught to pray, it's clear that action must follow.

As we pray 'hallowed be your name' we may wonder which name in particular, as God is given many different names in the Bible, each with its own significance. Well, you could take any biblical name for God and pray around that and it would be very profitable. However, I want to pass on to you the list of names that aids my prayer enormously.

That list starts with the name that God called himself to Moses, in Exodus 3:14: 'I AM'. It comes from the Hebrew *Yahweh*. It is the promised name of God. This name of God, because (by Jewish tradition) it was too holy to voice, is actually spelt *YHWH* without vowels. It is derived from the Hebrew word *Hayah*, which means 'to be'. This name is better known to us as *Jehovah*. So when we use the name *Jehovah* we are saying that God is who he is all the time – he never changes. That is surely one of the foundational truths of our faith.

In the Bible there are many names for God that begin with *Jehovah*, followed by one of his characteristics. Therefore, if we use those names, we know that the Father we're praying to is and will be that to us. For instance, if we take what is perhaps the best known, *Jehovah Jireh* – which means 'the Lord will provide', we are saying that we trust him to provide for us. It's like a blank cheque, signed by Father God, where we can fill in the amount – in this case not money, but the promise inherent in one or more of the *Jehovah* names that follow – and in faith claim that promise for ourselves and/or others.

So it's as if the Father is giving me a blank cheque. He has promised to honour it – I AM – and is saying, in effect, 'What do you need me to be for you today?' To complete the illustration, it is as if I fill in the amount. Then, as I pray, I'll take one or more of the Hebrew names of God and use them as requests for me, my family, friends, situations, etc.

So with that as the foundation, let's look at this list of eight *Jehovah* names. We'll take the Hebrew name (the spellings differ slightly, according to which source you use, but I'll use the simplest), then the English meaning followed by a biblical reference:

Jehovah Jireh – The Lord Will Provide – Genesis 22:14. God is our provider in all sorts of ways and it's his provision we need day by day. (Often humorously remembered as Jehovah Giro.)

Jehovah Rophe – The Lord Who Heals – Exodus 15:26. God is the healer of physical, emotional and spiritual problems. This book cannot go into the mystery of healing (why some people seem to be miraculously healed and many aren't), but the one thing we know is that the Father is the source of all healing.

Jehovah Shalom – The Lord Is Peace – Judges 6:24. This peace is not an absence of strife or difficulty, but an all-round welfare of body, mind and spirit. It also speaks of peaceful relationships, whether between two people or in a larger corporate setting. When you have time, research the Hebrew word *shalom*. It's full of meaning and I can't do it justice here.

Jehovah Rohi – The Lord My Shepherd – Psalm 23:1. This may not be the best-known Hebrew name, but is surely the best-known one in English. What a wealth of meaning lies here! In order to fully appreciate what the Father's shepherding is all about you need to read the whole Psalm. Let me say here that Marion (my wife) and I have lived in the good of this Psalm for many years and found it to be of great comfort and challenge. In my time as a church leader, I've often used it with others also. In many ways, I'd love to open it up here, but that's not the purpose of this book.

Jehovah Nissi – The Lord My Banner – Exodus 17:15. The context of this verse is one where Israel had victory in battle over their enemies. The Lord was the banner under which the Israelite army fought. You'll have seen films, such as *Gladiator*, where the banner under which the army fights flies high. It represents the authority and power invested in the nation and its armies, and inspires the individuals fighting under it. God is still our banner toady, as we face all sorts of things which seem to come against us.

Jehovah Tsidkenu – The Lord Our Righteous Saviour – Jeremiah 23:6. This is surely the heart of the Gospel. In fact, the context of this part of Jeremiah is about the promise of a Saviour. Thank God that Jesus is our righteousness, because if we were to have to qualify for his eternal love and care by our own righteousness we'd be out in the cold.

Jehovah M'keddesh – The Lord Who Makes You Holy – Exodus 31:13. We'll never make ourselves what God wants us to be. If you've ever tried to you probably ended up frustrated and disappointed – and actually you can end up feeling worse. The Father is the one who make us holy, sanctifies us, sets us apart – the one who produces the spiritual fruit in us. (By the way, if you have problems remembering this name just think of the 'M'k' as 'Mc . . .' the Scottish Lord.)

Jehovah Shammah – The Lord Is There – Ezekiel 48:35. This name could also be translated as 'The Lord, the ever-present one'. The context in Ezekiel is of the rebuilding of Jerusalem. The Israelites were bereft when Jerusalem was destroyed – their security and sense of nationhood was gone. God's promise was that whatever happened he was always there. That name spoke of restoration. What a promise for us: his presence always with us and the certainty of restoration.

So those are the *Jehovah* names that I use as I pray this part of the People's Prayer.

Let me give you an example. I may sense as I'm praying that I really need God's provision. Remember here that we started this book by stating that we are praying to our Father, so as we face the need for provision we know that a loving Father wants to provide. So I pray, 'Father, be *Jehovah Jireh* to me today. I take that promise that you've made.' Then I might realise that Marion is facing a particular situation that day, so I'll then pray, 'And Father, be *Jehovah Nissi* to Marion today and protect her under your banner.'

So we have honoured the name of the Father as we pray, and we have prayed for ourselves and others using the names of God. But don't forget that we must follow up our prayer by taking opportunities to practically honour his name day by day.

6
KINGDOM MATTERS
─⁄⁄⧵─

I mentioned in the last chapter about this prayer having an order, and in Chapter 3 showed that order (Fig. 1) as being first man's heart open to God, then God's heart open to man.

Imagine one of the film scenes you've probably seen a number of times, where a man is telling his wife/partner/lover that he loves her. He goes for one of those slightly dramatic holds – one hand behind her back, one hand on her stomach, leaning her back slightly – and says, 'You are the most beautiful woman in all the world and I love you with a passionate, undying love.' He then stands her upright, pats her on the backside and says, 'Now run along. I'll have baked beans on toast for lunch and, by the way, I'd like a new set of golf clubs for my birthday.' She would be forgiven for responding, 'You've just told me how you love me. How about asking what I'd like rather than telling me what you'd like?'

Crazy! And yet much of our praying can be like that: we can worship for a bit and then launch straight into a list of requests. Sometimes we may not worship at all, but just make requests. The People's Prayer won't allow that. You can't possibly go straight from honouring the name(s) of Father God in a worshipful way and telling him how you love him, to asking that he would give us our daily bread. Why?

Because *prayer preserves God's interests before it takes care of mine.* So after honouring his name we say, *'your kingdom come, your will be done, on earth as it is in heaven.'* Don't forget that even as we've prayed 'hallowed be your name,' we've been concerned with God's concerns because we've been asking that it should happen on earth as it is in heaven. So we've already started to ask for the things on his heart. Now it's about his kingdom and will.

Firstly, *'your kingdom come [on earth as it is in heaven]'*. I'm sure you know a lot about the Father's kingdom, but let's remind ourselves so we know what we're praying for. When we speak about kingdoms in this world, we are speaking about places, geographical territory. But God's kingdom is a presence, not a place. It's wherever God is 'kinging' it. We're not asking that he sets up a government in the UK or America or any other country – a kind of Christian political party – but that his kingly presence and power are known throughout the world. What we're in effect asking is that our Father's character and qualities become the ruling character and qualities in this world in which we live.

It's important to emphasise again here that this prayer always uses 'our' and 'we', so as we pray about his kingdom and will we are not praying selfishly. This part of our praying can take the longest. I don't mean by that that you should measure how long you take praying this part compared to the rest. None of what I'm writing is meant to convey that spirituality is measured in the length of our prayer times. What I mean is that God's kingdom and will are such vast areas that this part of the prayer gives us the opportunity to pray about so much.

Remember the index praying that has been helpful to many in keeping their minds from wandering, so that at any stage of our praying we remember where we've got to. Now at this stage I'm including everything to do with the Father at work in my life and way beyond.

I want to make here what I suppose could be seen as a bold statement: prayer is not for wimps, but for warriors! I see the People's Prayer, especially at this point, as courageous declarations, not hopeful requests. When we pray, 'your kingdom come, your will be done,' we're not being typically British with a polite request: 'Please would you increase your kingdom presence here. A lot of it would be wonderful, but even a little would do.' No! The thrust of these phrases is 'Come, your kingdom!' 'Be done, your will!' They are basically commands – issued by us because our longing is precisely that. I picture this part of the prayer as a person (the pray-er) putting their foot down hard, raising their fist in that 'Come on!' way and declaring, 'Come, your kingdom!' 'Be done, your will!' In effect we're saying, 'We've had enough of the kingdom of darkness; we've had enough of the ways of this world; we want to see things done your way.'

Some honest soul-searching must happen here, however. Have you ever asked yourself whether you really mean what you're praying about? I have, on a number of occasions. The thoughts tend to come tinged with guilt, which is never helpful, but come they do, such as 'Do I really want such-and-such to happen? If it did I'd have to sort a few things out in my life.' We can then try to justify our praying about whatever it might be by thinking that deep down, of course that's what we want. I'm sure these things are common to many, many Christians, and I'm also sure that it doesn't mean we're failures in the Father's eyes. Never forget that our heavenly Father understands that we are earthly beings who are on a journey to be more like Jesus, and that journey is not straightforward.

However, as you know, we can never let it rest there. We know innately that we cannot settle for less than the best. So we need, in the right way, to do some soul-searching. Do we really want his kingdom to come? Yes, certainly. But how about when his kingly rule interrupts our lifestyle, our desires and habits? The only reason I'm introducing this is that the more we know we mean what we're praying about, the more passionately we'll pray. Also it's a challenge to us – and that's never a bad thing. What I don't want to do here, though, is discourage you, so please don't stop praying because you know you might have some things to sort out. In fact, it's often as we pray that the Spirit will highlight anything that needs to be dealt with.

So, back to *'your kingdom come'*. Don't forget that we're praying that his kingdom will come on earth as it is in heaven. What do we imagine God's perfect heavenly kingdom to be like? There's no way that we can study that subject in any depth in a page or two here, but we can note a few things. We can say, based on what we read in Scripture, that it's a kingdom of love, absolute love. It's a kingdom where the authority of the king is complete and never questioned; that there's no rebellion. We can be sure that it's a kingdom where there are no prejudices against particular groups of people. We know that in his kingdom there will be no pain and no tears. We can be certain that there will be no injustice. You could think of many other things, but these will suffice for now.

Therefore, when you are stating that you want his kingdom to come, you need have no doubt that you can pray for these things to be present here on earth as well. It is important to make clear at this point that his kingdom will not be perfectly seen and experienced until Jesus comes back again, as he has promised to do.

There is a school of thought that holds to the belief that references to his kingdom are eschatological in nature – in other words, they're all about the future. But there seems enough evidence in Scripture to support the claim that we can work and pray for that kingdom, at least in part, in the here and now. You may have heard the expression 'the now and not yet kingdom' and that's precisely what it's about.

We pray this part of the prayer because we want to see the kingly rule of Jesus more and more here in this world, and we also pray that Jesus will return and establish his full and perfect kingdom. Right at the end of the Bible, in Revelation 22:17–20, we read, *'The Spirit and the bride say, "Come!" . . . Amen. Come, Lord Jesus!'* The bride is the church, and as you and I pray for his kingdom, so we join with the Spirit and the rest of the church in space and time in that biblical cry. I can honestly say that I have never been motivated as much as I am now to pray that prayer, longing to see Jesus return so that we can live in a kingdom of love, peace and justice. What a day that will be!

Let me give some practical tips about praying this part of the prayer. Firstly, as I intimated earlier, we must remember that we are including ourselves in this – that we want to see his kingdom in our own lives. It would be hypocritical to long for the kingdom everywhere, but not in my life. I find it helpful to act out what I'm praying, so I often stand on a particular spot and draw an imaginary circle around me, which signifies the Father's kingdom. I reach out my hand towards the edge of that circle, signifying that I want my life to be lived within his kingdom principles. If I reach out beyond the circle, I've acted outside of Jesus being Lord of my life. You can imagine that I'm often challenged as to my lifestyle!

After that, you can pray about anything you like. In fact anything that you have time for or make time for. This is the ideal place to pray for family, friends, church, community, and any national and international issues. It's here that you remember what was said earlier about what his kingdom is like. So we pray for love, peace, justice and all the other great qualities of that kingdom. We're praying that we'll see the presence of Jesus in our family, church, nation and nations. Be specific, not vague. Yes, we can pray simply for his kingdom, but it's so much more meaningful and effective to voice what we want to see, what we long for. One of the joys of praying specifically is seeing the answers to those prayers.

When praying about major issues it's easy to be discouraged because we can go from month to month or year to year and ostensibly see nothing change. This is where we need the courage of our convictions, namely that God hears and answers prayer. Stick at it! If future generations see the answers, so be it. As you do, expect to hear the Father calling you to be part of the answer. It's almost impossible to pray passionately about important things, be they to do with our own family or world matters, and never sense God speaking to us about how we can be involved – or indeed coming to the conclusion ourselves that we must get involved somehow.

7
YOUR WILL, NOT MINE
~•~

'Be done, your will!' That's what we pray in the next part of the prayer, as more literally translated from the original. Don't forget either that the implicit meaning is 'be done, your will, on earth as it is in heaven.' So, just as with praying about his kingdom, we are basically commanding. Not commanding God, but commanding his will to be done.

Once again, it's a very strong prayer. It's expressing that the only way we want the world to operate is in accordance with his will. Obviously one moment spent thinking about that line will bring the realisation that it's a huge prayer which, if and when answered would provide a massive shift in world affairs.

I can hear myself thinking, 'If that were really possible, and people have been praying this ever since Jesus taught the prayer, why is the world still as it is? What's the point?' Again, that's where we need a sense of perspective: that our prayer joins with prayers prayed over the centuries, and over those centuries, many major issues have been overturned. Obvious examples are the tearing down of the Iron Curtain, the Parliamentary bill passed in Wilberforce's day to abolish the transatlantic slave trade, and the formal end of apartheid. It's our duty and privilege to pray, on our watch, that his will be done, even if the answers come beyond our lifetime.

I want to introduce here one of the problems associated with 'your will be done'. I think most of us have, at one time or another, heard people tacking 'if it's your will' on to the end of a prayer. And then also heard someone say that it's lacking faith to say 'if it's your will' and that in fact it's a kind of get-out clause for God – really meaning that it's a get-out clause for us in case the prayer doesn't seem to be answered. And you can see why. If I pray for something and it doesn't seem to happen then I can say that it wasn't God's will. The problem is that it's not necessarily untrue. If God is God then we must allow him to have his way. Yes, but can our prayers not be more full of faith so that we don't need a get-out clause? And why are we taught to pray 'your will be done'?

As I've thought about this over the years of studying the People's Prayer, I've held on to a picture that I had. I saw a crowd of people making their way towards a large building. From what I could see, it was a building which God inhabited, and the people were obviously approaching the Father because they had things they wanted to ask of him. In other words, it was about praying. Most of the people stopped before the building, dropped to their knees and began praying, as if being a little wary of getting right into God's presence. But as I watched I saw some of the people going through the door, and it was only then that I realised that written in capital letters over the door were the words 'MY WILL BE DONE'.

I found that puzzling, but fairly soon realised what it was about: most of the people hadn't really thought about what it meant to submit to God's will and stopped short of that, preferring to ask for what they wanted and hope for the best. But those who entered the building wanted, with all their heart and soul, to submit to their Father's will, whatever that might be. I understood that I was being taught that we can pray in faith and do not need a get-out clause, and yet we need to accept God's will, because we are determined to follow him and know his will is best. So that means that I don't need to attach 'if it's your will' to the end of my prayer, but I do need, if I sincerely believe it, to be prepared to say 'your will be done'. The greatest example of this is Jesus, who in the Garden of Gethsemane before his crucifixion cried out to his Father, *'yet not my will, but yours be done'* (Luke 22:42).

This is more pertinent to praying for our own situations than national or international ones, where the Father's will is usually plain to see, and we'll look at that soon. But it's in our own situations where we often wonder whether we're praying with selfish motives, and this is understandable.

I've been concentrating on praying about God's will in our own lives and situations, and that's one part of our praying in this section. Once again, it proves just how great this prayer is, that it allows us to pray for the Father's guidance: one of the biggest issues about which people seek counsel. It seems that many people find it difficult to discern God's will for their lives, and I can understand why. I think that if we want to please God, we're so concerned about not getting it wrong that we feel we need absolute clarity, and that seems difficult to find.

I want to take a few moments to offer a little advice on this point. From the many times that I've counselled people looking for clarity on God's guidance for their lives, be it jobs, relationships, churches, moving house, or whatever, I find most are hoping for a ready-packaged answer that covers all the details.

Occasionally that happens, but most of the time it doesn't.

Let's take the example of someone who is sensing a call to serve God in a more full-time way, and they ask me to help them find out what that might be. My advice is always to ask God for a starting point. For instance, is there a sense that they are to serve overseas or in their home land? Is it with young people, the elderly or families? Is it likely to be mostly a teaching, pastoral or evangelistic ministry?

As I said, usually God's guidance doesn't come in one go. If it did, how would faith grow? No, we need to discover what God is saying and trust his word. I'm not suggesting that it's a long, hard, complicated search – I suppose it's more like a treasure hunt in which God is more than prepared to lead us to the next step. But we have to start somewhere and the theoretical situation I'm outlining is no different. So I would suggest to this person that they should pray for at least one element to be clear, and the rest will follow. There's one other important thing as well, and that is that any guidance will almost always resonate with the individual's gifting or passion or a sense of rightness in their life. Hopefully that will help if you are seeking his will in your own life.

However, praying that God's will be done in our life is only part of praying this phrase of the People's Prayer. Remember that in this prayer we are mainly praying in the plural ('us' not 'me'), and we use this phrase to call for God's will to be done on the earth. I'm sure I don't need to outline the many ways in which groups of people or nations make decisions and act contrary to his will. After all, it's the essence of why the world is as it is – because God's perfect will has been abandoned and people make their own sinful, selfish choices. So, as I said earlier, this is a massive prayer.

So, where to start praying for God's will to be done on earth? Surely, with the issues that are most on your mind – the things that trouble you most. You can pray with most heartfelt passion about those things. Karl Barth, the great German theologian, is attributed with saying, 'Read the Bible in one hand and the newspaper in the other.' Someone wisely used that as a basis for saying, 'Pray with the Bible in one hand and the newspaper in the other.' Most of the national and international issues where we long to see God's will done are in the news and his will is made plain in the Bible.

At this point, let me mention something about Bible reading. I find it best and most helpful to combine praying the People's Prayer with reading the Bible. As I pray about the Father's kingdom and will – in fact any part of the prayer – I'm informed, inspired, encouraged or challenged by what I've read. That can happen whichever is your preferred method of reading: whether it's your own Bible study or if you're using one of the many available aids to Bible reading. Often I find that what I've just read forms the basis of my subsequent praying.

Here's one example. I read Psalm 23, all about God as the Shepherd. The encouragement in that psalm starts with, '*The Lord is my shepherd*' and continues throughout, even giving us hope when facing the most difficult of situations. When I then started praying the People's Prayer that psalm formed the background to my prayer time. So, for instance, when praying and praising God as Father, I included the fact that he is our shepherd as well. When praying about his name, I was immediately inspired to use one of the Hebrew names for God, *Jehovah Rohi*, the Lord My Shepherd (see Ch. 5), as I prayed for my family. For example, 'Be a shepherd to Marion and my family today.'

The psalm also informed my praying for his kingdom to come and will to be done as I realised that so many of the world's ills begin because people don't have anyone who is like a caring shepherd to them. Jesus is recorded as saying in Matthew 9:36, '*When he saw the crowds, he had compassion on them, because they were harassed and helpless, like sheep without a shepherd.*' So I could think of situations where people needed shepherding and, because God's will is to be the Good Shepherd to all people, could pray with energy that his will be done in those situations.

This is just one example, but as you combine reading Scripture with praying you will be pleasantly surprised at how many times your reading will aid your praying. What also comes from this combination is that your faith will rise, as it always does when we know it's God's word.

As I pray this phrase, it's very similar to praying for his kingdom to come. That is, after praying about his will and guidance in my own life I open it up to the family, the church of which I'm part, the local community, then national and international issues. I'm not suggesting here, by the way, that you have to go through all this every day. Obviously it's your choice, but you might want to concentrate on one thing one day and another aspect on another day. Through all this, please remember that the whole point of what I'm writing in this book is designed to be helpful and releasing in your prayer life, not increasing the sense of struggle.

As I've already said, we can see this prayer as having two halves: man's heart open to God and God's heart open to man.

We now move on in the next chapter to seeing God's heart open to us as we begin to pray about our own needs.

8
HOW ABOUT MY NEEDS?

I wrote earlier that prayer preserves God's interests before it takes care of mine. I believe that so far in the People's Prayer we have been praying about the Father's interests: that his name is honoured, his kingdom comes and his will is done, all of them on earth as in heaven. Now we are able to express those things that would be seen as our interests.

However, we must bear in mind that just as God's interests have become our interests, so our interests are shared by our Father. So we're not pleading with a God whose arm has to be twisted or who reluctantly feels he must hear us out, but a Father whose great love reaches out to us and wants to share our needs and burdens. How amazing that we can place our needs before a Father who has all authority in the heavens!

There are two words or phrases that, as I've studied this prayer, have surprised me by their absence or positioning. One of them is to do with sin, but I'll mention that in the next chapter. The other one is the word 'please'. Nowhere in this prayer does the word 'please' appear. I'm sure it's a word that you use in prayer. I know I do, despite what I'm about to say. 'Please' is a polite word, or a word used to make a request sound polite, but it can also be a wheedling or even begging word. As I write, I can almost hear a child asking hopefully for something which they know they're unlikely to be given, liberally sprinkling the request with 'please, please, oh please . . .' Each time the word gets more passionate and more drawn out. To be honest, I can almost hear myself doing the same thing, but trying to hide it better.

Naturally, we probably use 'please' in our praying, but the point I want to make is that a show of politeness is not going to impress God, and neither is wheedling or begging. This prayer is almost business-like (please hear me aright) in that Jesus has taught us to bring these things before God and expects us to get on and ask for them because he wants to answer them. We don't need to add the word 'please' in order to please God, if you'll pardon the pun.

The words found in Matthew 6:7 (NASB), *'And when you are praying, do not use meaningless repetition, as the Gentiles do, for they suppose they will be heard for their many words,'* apply somewhat to what we're saying here. Obviously there will be times when we're praying for something with real passion or urgency and will ask the same thing over and over. We do that naturally when there's an urgent personal or family need for instance, and I'm not saying that's wrong. What I'm trying to do here is to encourage you that God has heard the first time you ask and, I believe, takes it as seriously as asking repeatedly. As it says in Matthew 6:8, *'for your Father knows what you need, before you ask him.'* How amazing that we don't have to be polite or remember to say 'please'.

So we come to the first of the requests for ourselves: **'Give us today our daily bread,'** or 'Give us the bread we need for today.' I find this the most challenging of the requests, as most of us don't actually need to ask for daily bread, because we have quite enough coming in anyway. Perhaps we don't need to pray this phrase in the twenty-first century? On the other hand, you and I can think of many parts of the world where for starving people this would be the most urgent and important prayer. What then do we make of it?

Firstly, I believe that when praying this we are asking for more than food. We are asking for everything that we need in order to live that day, be it finance or help in some area of our lives. That certainly fits our situations meaningfully. But don't let's pass over the actual food part. One of the main things, as I've repeated on a few occasions, is that we're praying 'us' and 'our', so as we ask for daily bread we are asking that the needs of others, many of whom are in desperate need, are met.

Then I think the big one for us is to realise that all we have comes from God. So often we take so much for granted. Most of us have more than we need and, without thinking about it, we earn our money and spend it on whatever we want. This phrase of the prayer disciplines us to remember where all these things come from and consequently elicits our gratitude. A stark warning is made to the Israelites in Deuteronomy 8:17–18: '*You may say to yourself, "My power and the strength of my hands have produced this wealth for me." But remember the Lord your God, for it is he who gives you the ability to produce wealth.*' It's worth reading the entire chapter because it's a most important reminder that primarily we live by God's hand and generosity.

Let's look at our Father's character as we pray for our daily bread. Throughout Scripture we see that God is generous. So many times, in speaking about God and his ways, the writers use words like 'fullness', because that is his nature. We've already seen that one of God's names is *Jehovah Jireh*, our provider, so as we pray for daily bread we are taking him at his word.

We can also see this as God's life-support system. If we own a car, we'd be daft not to give it the fuel and oil that's necessary, or if we're gardeners, we'd be crazy not to water seeds and plants and add the necessary nutrients to the soil. We wouldn't own a pet and not feed it! Much more importantly, if God has made us, why would he not want to sustain us? Of course he does! Going back to Deuteronomy 8, we read an account of the manna that God sent when the Israelites were wandering around the desert with little food.

That's our Father's nature. We praise, worship and thank him for it. In 1 Kings 17, we read the account of Elijah, who in a time of drought was led by God to live by the brook Kerith from which he could drink, and was fed by ravens. Winged waiters! Fancy having birds spitting out bits of bread and meat by God's order just to keep you alive.

All our daily needs are met from the hand of God. One of the verses in Scripture I have to keep reminding myself of is Matthew 6:33: *'Seek first his kingdom and his righteousness, and all these things will be given to you as well.'* The 'things' referred to are material things. If we put God and his kingdom first (and we've already prayed in this prayer that we're determined to see his kingdom come), we will not be wanting for necessary sustenance. Perhaps a brief reminder is in order here: God has promised to provide for our needs, not our wants. Sometimes he gives us what we want, in addition to what we need, as a bonus – a gift out of his overflowing generosity.

It is important to underline the priority of seeking God's kingdom. I'm not playing with words or being super-spiritual. It sets our priorities right if we want to serve him. If we're longing for him to be King and bring in his kingly rule, then that's what we'll be looking for and living for. That means he will provide whatever daily bread we need, be it food, finance, or whatever is needed for living that kingdom lifestyle. If the kingdom sets our life's agenda, you can be certain that the King will ensure we have what we need to fulfil that.

For seven years, Marion and I lived by faith. To many, 'living by faith' is a well-known phrase, but maybe it isn't to you, so let me explain. What I mean is that we were reliant on God, trusting him for our income, because we were not in salaried employment. I'd read books about people who had lived by faith and was challenged to do the same, as we believed God had called me to leave my secular job in business and called us to take people who had problems into our home. I saw that some who were serving God in that kind of full-time capacity said they lived by faith, but actually lived by faith and hints. In other words, they hinted about their need for money and mentioned it in every letter and conversation.

I decided that we would neither drop hints nor ask for money. Actually, I got a bit too pedantic about it, but was determined to look to God alone. I need to be honest here and say that those who did live with us were mostly on benefits, and so we knew we'd be unlikely to go hungry, as they had to contribute to the house expenditure for food, etc. But for any other personal and family needs, all our requests were made to the Father. On almost every front, it was a constant, 'Give us today our daily bread'. And God always provided! It was quite often miraculous – sometimes in major ways, though usually in fairly small ways, but miraculous nevertheless. So you can see how this part of the prayer was, and still is, very meaningful to us and how I can encourage you to make this request to the Father.

I believe, however, that there is something else important to say about this part of the prayer. I've just mentioned how we needed to trust God for our needs for those seven years. But actually, shouldn't we all be trusting him for all our needs all the time? Aren't we looking to him for the strength to live each day in order to earn the money we get? Aren't we looking to him to help us find a job or career, to find the right friendships, to know which church community to be a part of, to understand what special gifts he's given us in order to serve? In other words, we should be looking to him every day for the bread needed for that day. So let's purposely realise and express that on a daily basis.

It's a great reminder of what I said earlier in the chapter about realising that it is God who gives us the strength to live, work, make relationships, raise a family, etc. The problem is that we live as if it's us upon whom life depends – our energy, our skills, our intelligence and so on. We lose sight of dependence on God and, as a result, too often lose our first love for him because we are so focused on ourselves. I can't stress this enough. If you meet someone, usually from a developing nation or someone serving God in a mission situation, who is literally looking to him for their daily bread/daily needs, you will find also that person will have a close walk with him that shines through their conversation and behaviour.

So, before we move on, make up your mind to remember daily

that it's only by the Father's grace and generosity that you are alive at all, and purposely pray, 'Give us today our daily bread.'

9
FULLY FORGIVEN

I mentioned in the last chapter that there were two words or phrases which, as I've studied this prayer, have surprised me by their absence or positioning. I said that one of them is to do with sin, and that subject is what we find next in the People's Prayer, commonly known as, **'Forgive us our trespasses as we forgive those who trespass against us.'** So we come to forgiveness for sin.

What surprises me is that this doesn't come first in the prayer. It only surprises me because I've found myself often praying it at the beginning of my prayers, so I'm basing it on my own experiences, not on anything more objective. Let me explain. Time and time again in my struggling to be a person of prayer, I made promises to God that I would improve my prayer life. However, the very next morning, having set the alarm for an earlier time in order to pray, would press the 'snooze' button and either go to sleep again or feel too tired to give myself to prayer. Then when I did get to pray, I would approach the time feeling guilty. Also, there were many times when the first thing on my mind as I came to pray was something I'd done wrong – often being less than kind to Marion or the children.

So the almost inevitable start to the prayer was something like, 'Oh Lord, I'm so sorry that I've once again not kept my promise to pray' or, 'Oh Lord, please forgive me for the way I spoke to Marion'. The problem is that in starting like that, you spend a fair bit of time feeling guilty and wondering how God can forgive you when you keep on doing the same things. I would find myself going round in small circles reminding myself that God's grace and mercy are limitless, and then wondering whether, although knowing that, I'd actually gone too far this time. The result was that by the time I'd assured myself that I was forgiven and could begin to pray I'd run out of time and had to compress any meaningful prayer into a very few minutes.

Great, liberating news! Jesus didn't teach us to begin the prayer asking for forgiveness. Imagine this scene. A small boy bursts into his dad's presence and (using the kind of language with which we often think we should address God) says, 'Oh paternal parent, full of intelligence, charm and panache, I would ask thee to provide the financial wherewithal to purchase a conical-shaped wafer that containeth the substance known as ice-cream, because I wish to purchase the same.' And the father responds, 'I'm not interested in your requests son until you've apologised for all the things you've done wrong – to your mother, me, your sister, and the cat. Once you've done that I may give you the money.' It's possible that if there were something major that the boy had done wrong, the father would ask for an apology first, but my guess is that most fathers would give the money, knowing that pretty soon the strains of 'Greensleeves' would be heard, signifying that the ice-cream van was moving on.

So this is the liberating news. We don't have to start our praying by wallowing in our sin and guilt, and then finding that there's little time to go further. Yes, certainly we need to confess our sin, but Jesus teaches us that it takes its place later in the prayer. We approach our Father based on relationship and his grace and mercy. So many of us are constantly battling self-deprecation, and it plays right into the enemy's hands because it takes our eyes off God and keeps them firmly on ourselves. As I've pointed out, we start the prayer by focusing on Father God, not on us.

So, on with looking at this part of the prayer. The more accurate translation of this part is, as found in Matthew 6:12, *'And forgive us our debts, as we also have forgiven our debtors.'* The picture behind these words is obviously of money: that we owed a sum of money and couldn't pay it, so asked the person to whom we owed it if they'd let us off. The challenging bit that's added is that we say that we have let other people off paying money they owe us. The debt we owe to God is massive. He atoned for our sin and selfishness by living a life of perfection – something that is impossible for us to do. We understand that Jesus paid that debt for us.

In the table in Chapter 3, I use the words forgiveness/ relationships. I guess it's obvious, but because we're asking for forgiveness in the same way that we have forgiven others, then this part of the prayer prompts us to ensure that any problems in relationships are put right. Note again the words, 'Forgive . . . as we also have forgiven'. In Matthew 6 there are two statements made by Jesus – one before and one after the People's Prayer – that emphasise parts of the prayer itself.

The first one is, *'your Father knows what you need before you ask him'* (v.8). The second one is pertinent to the part of the prayer we're looking at now, *'For if you forgive other people when they sin against you, your heavenly Father will also forgive you.*

But if you do not forgive others their sins, your Father will not forgive your sins' (vv.14–15). This is very stark. Does it really mean what it says? Well, it must do, because we can't suggest that Jesus exaggerated or used empty words. What if someone has done something horrendous to me or my family – am I expected to forgive? In a word, yes!

I realise that can seem unreasonable and impossible, but we have to face what Jesus is saying. I think the thing to bear in mind when trying to forgive something major is that we are not being asked to like the person responsible, but to forgive them. The meaning of the word 'forgive' in the original Greek is to 'send away', 'send forth', 'release', 'set free'. That means that if we don't forgive, we keep the person who's wronged us imprisoned. They may possibly not feel that, but from our point of view, they're imprisoned in our unforgiveness, resentment, maybe even hatred. The problem is that we are then ourselves imprisoned in the feelings of resentment, hatred, etc. That kind of thing can sadly, if allowed to continue, give us (the one not forgiving) a *raison d'être*. It's a bit like a stalker who becomes obsessed with their own feelings towards the object of their desire.

Forgiveness releases the person who has wronged us and releases us as well. If it makes us feel any better we can also take at face value God's words, *'It is mine to avenge; I will repay'* (Rom. 12:19). It's also most important to remember, when struggling to forgive someone, that Jesus paid the price for our forgiveness long before we confessed our sin and wrongdoing. Our release had been paid for; we just need to receive it, through repentance and faith. Romans 5:8 reminds us that *'God demonstrates his own love for us in this: while we were still sinners, Christ died for us.'* So we never have to wonder whether or not God will choose to forgive, and whether release will come. We know that if we confess and repent, forgiveness will be immediate and full. In other words, we have a 'get out of jail free' card. However much someone else has wronged us, do we want that person to remain forever in the jail of our unforgiveness, whether or not there was punishment through the legal system? What if we, not just for ever, but for eternity, were kept imprisoned because God wouldn't forgive us?

I realise that for quite a number of people this is a massive thing to have to do. I'm not for one moment suggesting that a person should just utter words of forgiveness to be on the safe side. That would be false. You need to be real about it, and it could well take a long time before you can manage it. So how can we deal with wrong done to us – something that is an offence against us? I want to build some advice around four words: 'owe', 'no', 'blow', 'sow'. Let me explain.

Firstly, **owe**: when someone has wronged us we feel they owe us something, at least an apology, and then we can forgive. But as we've seen, forgiveness is a command, and we're asked to forgive before we receive what we feel people owe us. That's what is so forceful in the words, *'And forgive us our debts, as we also have forgiven our debtors.'* They no longer owe us anything because we've forgiven them. So the first thing we need to come to terms with is that this person doesn't owe us anything.

Secondly, **no**: when someone has wronged us, we often mull over the wrong; we let it simmer in our minds. We might even rehearse in our most private thoughts what we'd like to see happen to the person – and it wouldn't make friendly reading! If we allow the offence to keep its place in our thoughts and lives, it's going to grow. We give it the soil of our headspace and water it by dwelling on it, and the result is quite possibly that something grows out of all proportion. So when that offence comes calling on us to turn it over in our minds again, we say, 'No, I won't entertain it!' and we keep saying that until it dies away.

Thirdly, **blow**: we need to go one further than saying no. We need, if you like, to blow it away. If the offence, or wrong, keeps haunting us, we have to go as far as cursing it. The situation might demand us being as tough as that. It's like having something in our hand and not wanting it there. We have the choice of holding on to it or throwing/blowing it away. That definite act can help us know that we've dealt with it.

Lastly, **sow**: we can choose to sow blessing or good things into the person who wronged us. This is not a command, although Jesus telling us to love our enemies and do good to those who mistreat us might be saying the same thing. It certainly would be an act of finality as far as dealing with a wrong is concerned. It would be following the Father's example of showing grace and mercy to us – not only forgiving us, but also pouring out good things on us.

So by praying this part of the prayer we are maintaining healthy relationships with others as well as knowing the Father's forgiveness. Think how often people annoy you. Sorry, that should read, I can think how often people annoy me – and how often I annoy others! Surely we know how quickly that annoyance can build up. A small annoyance with someone, when not dealt with, can become a dislike of that person. If we allowed too many of those to run free we'd end up with a fairly long list of people we don't get on with. The well-known advice is to keep short accounts, to settle things quickly – and that is most often just sorting ourselves out, not necessarily talking with the other person. Of course, it may be that something does need to be sorted face-to-face with someone else, but hopefully we have the wisdom and discipline to know when.

In summary then, as we pray this part of the prayer it might take a lot of courage and persistence (because it could take us a long time to get to grips with forgiving), but it will be so worth it. And how amazing it is that the Father is prepared to forgive us!

10
FIGHTING FIT
~⁄ı∖~

'And lead us not into temptation, *but deliver us from the evil one,'* is the last part of the People's Prayer. 'Hang on,' I hear some saying, 'there's more!' Ok, all will be revealed later.

What a strange thing to hear Jesus teaching that we should pray not to be led into temptation, as if God is just waiting to pounce on us and take us down temptation's road. A God who sets booby traps? Well, one translation of this part of the prayer says, 'Do not bring us to the point of the test,' and that is much more the meaning of this verse. It's a bit like a child who's been told how dangerous it is for her to go near the edge of the cliff saying to her parent, 'Don't lead me to the edge of the cliff.' It is ridiculous to contemplate that she'd need to tell her parent that! But how about that child saying, 'Don't let me go near the edge of the cliff'? That makes a lot of sense, because the child is aware of the danger, even though the parent would probably not do such a thing anyway.

Think about this before you pray this part. You alone know where temptation lies as far as your life is concerned, so as you pray this you're confessing that these temptations are too strong for you to counter with ease. You're saying, in effect, 'Father, don't let me get near that temptation.' One illustration I've often thought of whilst studying this prayer is of the Bermuda Triangle

– that loosely defined region in the western part of the North Atlantic Ocean, where a number of aircraft and ships are said to have disappeared under mysterious circumstances. Whether it's a real area or not, you can imagine captains and crew alike knowing the dangers of getting sucked into this area of water and saying to whomever, or to themselves, 'Whatever happens, don't let us get near the Bermuda Triangle.' They know they may not be able to control their vessel should it sail too close. You and I know that we may not be able to control ourselves if we get too near areas of temptation.

There's a promise in Scripture from which we can take courage in these situations: *'No temptation has overtaken you except what is common to mankind. And God is faithful; he will not let you be tempted beyond what you can bear. But when you are tempted, he will also provide a way out so that you can endure it.'* (1 Cor. 10:13). The original word for 'overtaken' is 'snatched'. In other words, it's often that sudden urge to give way to whatever temptation it might be. I'm sure you know what I mean – you're going about your daily life in the usual way, minding your own business, and suddenly temptation rears its head. If you give it a chance it'll develop quickly and, if you're anything like me, if you give it time to develop you'll find yourself giving in. But the promise is that there's an escape route, and I believe that to be the ability to turn our thoughts immediately to God and thereby step away from the temptation, or to remove ourselves immediately from the context of the temptation. It's our immediate response to temptation that counts.

Let's turn to the next phrase, ***'but deliver us from the evil one.'*** You probably learnt and usually pray this part as 'deliver us from evil', but the more accurate translation is 'evil one'. That makes sense, as evil is a general term, with no name or face (or possibly many names and faces where we see evil behaviour), and if that were the case we'd be praying that we be delivered from this 'thing'. Where would this 'thing' live? Do I know when it might strike or when I'm somewhere near it? Are there people who are permanently evil or are some people (perhaps including us) a mixture of good and evil? What would deliverance from this evil mean – that we never get anywhere near it? Surely that could never be guaranteed!

No, our prayer is for deliverance from the evil one. In our understanding and from Scripture, we believe that to be Satan. In 1 Peter 5:8 we read, *'Be alert and of sober mind. Your enemy the devil prowls around like a roaring lion looking for someone to devour.'* That's the deliverance for which we're praying: that we don't fall prey to this evil one. I've been watching one of the BBC's great wildlife programmes recently. It's called *The Hunt*, and there's been the usual excellent film footage of predator and prey. One of the things that you continually notice is that the hunters, especially the big cats, often have to single out the weaker prey or the young, or those on the edge of the herd. Surely the same is true of our enemy – that the weak in faith or the unguarded are much easier pickings. Also, those who try to live as Christians independently, with little or no place in a local church, are vulnerable, like the animals on the edge of the herd. That's why this part of deliverance links so closely to the bit on temptation – so that we're aware and on our guard.

I have to say I find this phrase as puzzling as the first phrase in this part of the prayer. Why do we need to ask God to deliver us from the evil one? Doesn't he want to do that anyway without us asking? Is he unaware of what might be happening to us, so we have to shout for help in case he hasn't noticed, or at least remind him of the problem? Isn't that why Jesus came – to destroy all the works of the evil one?

Those are reasonable questions, but a lot of this prayer follows the same pattern. *'Give us today our daily bread.'* Isn't God our provider anyway? *'Your kingdom come, your will be done.'* If God is God then surely he can make that happen anyway. But if he were to do all these things without our involvement in asking, we would be merely automatons. Surely this prayer is an exercise in faith: knowing that God is willing to fulfil all the things contained in it and therefore co-operating with him and trusting him. In Hebrews 11:6 we read that *'without faith it is impossible to please God'*. Here then is faith in action!

This also applies to *'deliver us from the evil one.'* I sometimes wonder how many of us ever pray that. I never used to pray that except when involved, on a few occasions, in deliverance ministry (setting people free from troubling spirits). I have to confess that I often still don't, and actually, as I write this I'm challenged to practise what I write.

I've often asked myself the question: if prayer is important and God answers it, what happens if we don't pray what God has asked us to pray? In other words, is praying *'deliver us from the evil one'* merely 'the right thing to say', or is it a necessity? If it's not a necessity, why pray it? Do you see what I mean? Let me attempt an answer. Firstly, I don't think we take the enemy of our souls very seriously. We tend to place any kind of emphasis on the devil at the feet of those on the slightly whacky side of the church but, whilst there certainly can be an unhealthy emphasis, to ignore his very real wiles is foolishness. Secondly, as we pray this part we are reminded of the real dangers of falling into the devil's clutches, and as a result, we should become more watchful and aware.

There's a very interesting statement made by Jesus to Peter in Luke 22:31–32: *'Simon, Simon, Satan has asked to sift all of you as wheat. But I have prayed for you, Simon, that your faith may not fail.'* I immediately wonder why Jesus didn't say, 'But I won't allow him to sift you.' After all, Jesus could have done that easily – he has the authority! But all he does is pray for Peter that his faith will remain intact. If Jesus prayed for the disciples regarding the work of the enemy, then surely we need to pray for ourselves. Could it be that we suffer at the enemy's hands because we don't think it's all serious enough to pray about?

It wouldn't be right to leave this section of the prayer without thinking about other ways of resisting the works of the evil one, and there's nothing more pertinent than the passage about the armour of God, found in Ephesians 6:10–18. The second verse of that passage is quite clear, *'Put on the full armour of God, so that you can take your stand against the devil's schemes.'* It surely links clearly to what we're praying when we say, *'deliver us from the evil one.'* It's quite clear that much of the answer to this lies in our own hands.

Some writers and preachers advocate imagining putting on this armour daily as we pray. That might be a real help to you and, if so, take the time to do it. But that might not be up your street, as it were. The important thing is to realise the truth of what this passage of Scripture teaches and to ensure our obedience to the wisdom contained there. As it seems that Jesus taught us to pray this prayer daily ('give us today our daily bread'), it seems sensible to check as we pray that these pieces of armour are in place on us.

Let's look at these pieces of armour and, as you do, check out whether you're leaving parts of yourself vulnerable to attack. All vital organs are covered by this armour: those in the head, chest and middle regions. It is designed to guard our thoughts, heart and emotions. As well as the defensive armour, it also gives us a weapon for attack and the footwear needed to make proper progress in the battle.

We'll start from the head and work down, rather than taking the pieces in the order they appear in the passage. Firstly the *'helmet of salvation'* (v. 17). Surely this is protection for our thoughts, knowing that the Father has saved us and that we belong to him. So many of our problems stem from that doubt about God's unfailing love for us and our own unworthiness. I mentioned in Chapter 9 that we can spend too much time dwelling on our own sin and subsequent concern as to whether God really does go on forgiving us. This helmet of salvation should cover all those thoughts and produce, through faith, a certainty that we belong to the Father. With this helmet we deflect the devil's whispers about whether or not we're saved and whether we're worthy enough.

Then the *'breastplate of righteousness'* (v. 14). The most important part of this seems to me to cover our heart, the seat of our love and emotions. What and whom do we love? Is our love for the Father being expressed in right living? Are we setting up a guard against the lusts that so easily beckon us in their direction?

This righteousness firstly derives from who Jesus is – that he's our righteousness. So as we stay close to him we find the desire to live right keeps growing and, when temptation comes, we can make the right choices.

After this, and actually coming first in this passage from Ephesians, is *'the belt of truth'* (v. 14). This piece of armour holds everything else in place, which is why I guess it's placed first in the order. Without truth everything else can fall apart. It's the truth about God, Jesus and the Holy Spirit, the truth about our salvation, and the truth about ourselves – knowing ourselves, our strengths and weaknesses, our gifts and abilities. When we disbelieve what God has done for us and our standing in him, and when we reckon we're a whole lot better than we really are and think we can do things that we're really not gifted to do, we're so vulnerable to the devil's attacks, because we're not being truthful and are believing lies. That weakens us considerably, and you can see how the other parts of the armour could become loose and ineffective.

'The shield of faith' (v. 16) is the main part of our defence. A little earlier in this chapter, we looked at Hebrews 11:6: *'without faith it is impossible to please God'*. The whole Christian life is a life of faith – faith that our sins have been forgiven, that God loves us unconditionally, that he goes on loving even though we go on stumbling and failing. The picture I get is of the Roman soldier lifting his shield into the right position to block the arrows being shot. In such a way, we meet the arrow whispers and temptations of the enemy, by standing in faith in the areas where we're being targeted.

The verse we're looking at says that with this faith we're able to extinguish all the flaming arrows of the evil one. Those were prime offensive weapons used by the Roman armies – not just arrows, but arrows soaked in flammable liquid and set alight. If the arrow didn't pierce you, the fire would begin to burn. What a warning for us as the enemy fires the arrows: that whilst the temptation or whisper may not pierce us, we can be somehow 'burnt' by what's happened. But the shield of faith puts out the fire.

Let's have a brief look at *'the sword of the Spirit, which is the word of God'* (v. 17). In one way, the picture of the soldier with a shield in one hand and sword in the other helps us understand this, because faith and God's word go together. In what is our faith placed? Yes, in God, but very much in his word. Often our faith will express itself by quoting the word of God. It strengthens our faith and repels the evil one. Remember how Jesus used God's word when being tempted by Satan in that wilderness experience.

Finally, we have the footwear, *'feet fitted with the readiness that comes from the gospel of peace'* (v. 15). The standard military footwear of the republican and early imperial Roman army was the 'caliga', a sort of nailed sandal. So the shoe was a sandal, giving great flexibility of movement – necessary because trainers were not available! The nails in the sole would give good, firm grip over muddy terrain. Almost immediately, you can see the analogy: we need to be ready to share the gospel or the impact of the gospel in our lives.

But why is this listed as a piece of armour in its spiritual context? You can see how the others relate, but the footwear is not so obvious. I think there's a twofold answer: firstly, being ready with the gospel is taking the fight to the enemy. We're spreading light in the darkness; bursting through the enemy's ranks, flying the banner of Jesus. Secondly, being ready with the gospel necessitates our staying close to God and thus maintaining a righteous lifestyle, which gets right up the devil's nose.

There is, however, one more thing to comment on before leaving this passage on armour in Ephesians, and that is prayer (vv. 18–20). This passage ends with the very theme of this book. In verse 18 we are told to pray in the Sprit and at all times. And that's exactly why I've written this book – to help anyone who chooses to read it to nurture a prayer life which is both meaningful and delightful.

Go on, pray the way that Jesus taught!

Before finishing, I must explain briefly why I haven't written a chapter on the last sentence of the well-known prayer. My explanation follows as a PS.

PS
⌐╱╲⌐

'For yours is the kingdom, the power and the glory for ever and ever.' Yes, it really is a PS! These words don't appear in most of the older manuscripts. It's thought that they were added later – as a fitting postscript to what had gone before. And that's why you won't find them in the NIV.

Having said that, it is a great way to end this prayer, as we state God's sovereignty for all time and eternity. They are words to which we can give a hearty 'Amen', so we can use them freely. No follower of Jesus and child of the Father would disagree with what has been added. In fact, as we pray this People's Prayer, we can finish on this note of praise. It may have been thought that the prayer shouldn't finish with the accent on deliverance from the evil one, but rather turn again to praise and worship the Father in the way it started.

May the Father enrich you as you desire to be a person of prayer, move through the discipline, and find prayer to be a delight.

⌐╱╲⌐

I've summarised the main points of the Prayer so that you can have something simple to hand as a resource for your own prayer times. You can print out the sheet at:

http://www.lifechurchwilmslow.org/teach-us-to-pray